Mandela:

Echoes of Apartheid
and Impunity

Mandela:
Echoes of Apartheid and Impunity

Chronological Predictions and Fulfillments

Dr Sam Iheanacho Madugba

(**DPH**(*WAHEB*), **Dip-in-Env.Hlth**(SOHT,Aba), **MBBS**(*Nig*), **MPH**(*Nig*)
Public Health Physician & Director of Public Health
Ministry of Health
Owerri. Imo State, Nigeria.

(Winner, Association of Nigerian Authors, ANA,
Imo State Chapter's Award in Poetry, 2005 with the
book, *Nigeria: Buhari's Boots, Babangida's Boots*)

authorHOUSE®

AuthorHouse™ UK
1663 Liberty Drive
Bloomington, IN 47403   USA
www.authorhouse.co.uk
Phone: 0800.197.4150

*Cover illustration done by Chikezie Chilaka (Peacemaker) as
well as the 4th, 6th(b), 7th, 8th, 9th, 10th and 11th inside the
book. 1st illustration was by Omenka Charles Okata while David
Kalu did 2nd, 3rd, 6th(a) and 13th illustration. The late Dr
Kennedy Okereke aka Iwuanyanwu drew the 5th figure*

Published by AuthorHouse   01/12/2015

ISBN: 978-1-4969-9443-1 (sc)
ISBN: 978-1-4969-9444-8 (e)

"There is a longing for freedom in every human heart, a longing that arises in response to events and situations that limit us, but not many of us can give vivid expression to this longing as Sam Madugba has done in his *Mandela : Echoes Of Apartheid And Impunity*, a contemporary treatise in verse which represents a personal odyssey on Nelson Mandela and Apartheid as well as a socio-political critique of unjust structures and practices of our society. His goal is to re-awaken in every one of his readers, if possible by force, the hunger for freedom, justice, responsibility, love and perfection."

-Rev Fr Gilbert Alaribe, Ph.D, Seat of Wisdom Major Seminary, Owerri, Nigeria.

In straddling the African socio-political landscape through three stages of maturation, Sam Madugba in his *Mandela: Echoes Of Apartheid And Impunity* has demonstrated an uncanny ability to maintain a passion-sustained focus so rare in distracting economies and tumbling social conditions that his country, Nigeria offers. This book compels attention. Now and again it reads like a lamentation which it is not. At other times, one gets the impression of a protest, but it is not one; yet sometimes, the poems read like a realistic offering, and they are not. The immediacy of the subject, the range of the linguistic vehicle, and the varied approach to the presentation of the theme invite a closer reading of the poems. Sam Madugba is indeed a poet of exceptional talent.

-Professor Toni Duruaku, Dept of English, Alvan Ikoku Fed.College of Education, Owerri.

''As long as the creative spark is kept alive so doggedly and fruitfully by individuals like you, there is hope for our Nigerian humanity."

Professor Wole Soyinka, 1993.

''Sam Madugba, even at his maiden incursion into poetry, manifests a singular vision and immense prophetic acumen, which may give his maiden volume immortality."
Professor Ernest Emenyonu, December 7, 1993.

'' Sam Madugba is a double genius, genius in Arts and genius in Science. He is prolific and immensely productive."
Professor Catherine Acholonu, December 7, 1993.

'' Sam Madugba is a phenomenon - a medical doctor with literary talents, ready to have fun, to bridge the gap between Science and Literature despite the morbidity that surrounds him."
Professor (Monsignor) Theophilus Okere, 2000

'' A rare combination"
- Dr Nnanna Ukegbu , TEDEM House, Imerienwe.

''*Mandela: Echoes of Apartheid And Impunity* is a work crafted by a man with a passionate heart for justice and human rights. It is an odyssey of sort, of horrendous events in Africa's recent past, her somersaulting present and of course, her precarious future which this book will certainly positively influence if Africans agree to read it and imbibe its lessons."
-Chidi Nkwopara, Editor, *The Vanguard,* Owerri, Nigeria.

''Sam Madugba's *Mandela: Echoes of Apartheid And Impunity* is a portrayal of human possibilities as long as divine intervention is not neglected. This charismatic Catholic physician and scholar has scored yet another excellent mark with this unprecedented modern work of arts, science and religion."
— Emeka Ani, Editor, *The Leader Catholic Newspaper,* Owerri, Nigeria.

To Nnamdi Azikiwe, Chukwuemeka Odumegwu-Ojukwu, Muhammadu Buhari, Thomas Sankara, Nnanna Ukegbu, Gani Fawehimni, Wole Soyinka, Chinua Achebe, Chima Ubani, Balarabe Musa, Abubakar Umar, Femi Falana, Oscar Romero, Anthony Olubumi Okogie, Anthony Obinna, Theophilus Okere, EAC Orji and Dennis Brutus who with Nelson Mandela, taught us how to rebel against tyranny and organized evil, and how to say no to lies accepted by all.

Acknowledgements

I heartily express my gratitude and that of my family to everybody, man or woman, who has contributed either positively or negatively to my life, my living, my survival on earth, my education and especially my little knowledge of things of God.

To my friends, admirers and positive contributors, I say thanks for making me realize that I am not totally bad. To my enemies, critics and negative contributors, I say you are welcome, as you make me know that I am not all good.

To the indifferent and those who do not know me, this tiny book of poems on our collective terrible experiences in Africa yesterday and today is an opportunity for them to further unveil my true identity, so that they can either love me, hate me, be or remain indifferent to me.

To my beautiful wife, Linda, my sweet children and their caretakers in past 17 years, I bow and tremble. To my mother who has remained sharp even in old age, I remain loyal. I mourn my father who died in the heat of my struggles in 2005.

To those who contributed to the writing and production of this particular book, especially Dr Mike Gbenga Ajileye, former Chairman, Association of Nigerian Authors, ANA, Imo State Chapter, who read through this work and made useful suggestions; our revered Professor (Msgr) Theophilus Okere, who agreed to write the preface; Professor ABC Duruaku, who did the foreword; Rev. Fr Dr Gilbert Alaribe, Emeka Ani and Chidi Nkwopara who wrote commentaries to this work, I am grateful.

I equally salute my loving brother and mentor, Dr Joe Goziem Nwaorgu, Professors Chidi Osuagwu, Ikechukwu Dozie and Isidore Diala; Rev. Frs. Victor Eleba, Christian (Little Angel) Eke, Chinedum Osuji, Protase Anyanwu; Sir Alex Ukaegbu, Sir A. Nonyelum , Mazi Fabian Agba, Matthew Mbakwem, Elly Eke, Drs. Marcel Azubuike, Obioms Iwuagwu, Chinwe Osuchukwu, George Udeji; Eze Ekenweke, Fabian Ajagba and Ujunwa Okereafor, among many others who always identify with me.

I equally recognize the contributions of my head nurse, Mrs Ifeyinwa Mmadike, my confidants and childhood friends, Area Manager and Joe Njoku, my personal assistants, Hon Ndubuisi Eke, Mrs Immaculata Ejiagwu, Engineer Nnamdi Izuawuba, Mr Henry Kekeocha, Engineer Mike Power Egejuru, and of course, Miss Vivian Onyinyechi Uba, my secretary, who painstakingly and happily did all the typing. I greatly commend my graphic artists, David Kalu Opara and Peacemaker Chilaka, and of course, my formidable attorney, Sir EEJ Agwulonu.

I cannot forget my kinsman, Emmanuel Ibe James, author of *Under Bridge* who linked me up to Charity Mondoy, my publishing consultant at AuthorHouse Publishers, London, who thankfully, guided me in this publishing process.

And to all those who will read this book, I wish them the constant realization that hardly has a life of silver-spoon, adulation and sycophancy had a glorious end. On the contrary, focused lives personified by deprivations, rejections, sufferings, pains, persecutions, perseverance and determination such as led by Christ, Mandela, Gani and the like, have never disappointed.

Dr Sam Iheanacho Madugba
Owerri, June 19, 2014.

Foreword

Mandela: Echoes Of Apartheid And Impunity is a collection of twenty six reflective poems that in many ways, postmark three key stages in the poet's life: student, employee, and passionate commentator on an African socio-political space; properly pigeon-holed in the iconic life of Nelson Mandela with whom the poet finds a common ground as a peace-means crusader.

This collection, brilliantly decorated with 13 explanatory illustrations, is in three sections, the first being shots of his impressions before he went to train as a medical doctor; Section B contains the poems of his medical school days while in Section C, his introspection matures during his medical practice period. So, one can easily title these sections Pre-, Intra-, and Post-medical training. Beyond these signposts however, Madugba ties little else, apart from his strong Christian sentiments, to the contents of his poems which he stoutly called: *Mandela: Echoes Of Apartheid And Impunity.*

Section A posts eight poems: "Apartheid: Chants of Liberation," a poem of 325 lines which reminisces the era in a clarity of a direct witness, although there is no certainty that the poet was directly involved in the South African experience. "The Misty Future" is a shorter, less evocative poem, somber and sober; almost despairing. "Your Voice Echoes" re-visits the revolutionary temper and tone, while "Their Game Spoils" although still on the theme, seeks succor from beyond this world, a divine intervention, perhaps? In "But For Noble Mosquito", the poet collapses the apartheid experience to the West

African sub-region that escaped the social malaise due to the barrier the mosquito provided. "With Them I Protest" is a pithy poem that adulates some freedom fighting 'Greats' across the globe. "Let's Let Loose" maintains the apartheid idiom. The poem is powerfully conciliatory, yet demanding on the need for unity to produce the best. In "I Dined With Africa", the poet returns to a celebration of Africa whose progress is stymied by multilingualism. Hear him:

> *Our tongues refused to rhyme*
> *Our breaths refused to resonate*
> *Twenty and one brothers together,*
> *Forty and two tongues apart.*

There are six poems in **Section B**: "My Friends", a salute to many Nigerian 'Greats', selected world leaders and some personal acquaintances. "The Thorn Here is Sharper" is a spiky poem which squares back to apartheid, but at the local level. In "And Mandela Persists," the poet returns to the primary thematic pre-occupation: Mandela's enduring convictions and inimitable spirit. This focus remains in the short poem, "Denials." In "I Look Beyond," the poet establishes a relationship between the challenges of his academic studies and the apartheid in South Africa. As one was overcome, so would the other be vanquished. In each case, the poet looks heavenwards. "Try A Visit Today" is introspective and sober. Although Mandela is mentioned to capture the spirit of the theme, and to emphasize the sacrifice in his incarceration, the poem is largely an advice to seek divine intervention in the affairs of men.

The twelve poems in **Section C** index the mature focus of the poet. The dithering in stance and tone of the first two stages are now over. In "And Mandela Emerges" the central Mandela theme re-appears strongly with a new verve. "And Mandela Ascends" projects the rejuvenation idiom of a Fall before a Rise. "A Passion To Intervene" is a Gani Fawehinmi eulogy echoing the travails of a social crusader. Concerned about a topical issue of his profession and surely inspired by his work at a HIV/AIDS Centre, "AIDS And Africa" addresses the scourge of the century which the poet blames on the scapegoat search for the smoking gun in Africa by the West. "The Unnormal Crusader" is a 226-line narrative of the persecutions the poet suffered in the hands of an African government that employed him and his survival strategies which he later in the following poem, "The Upright, His Ironies" confessed, woefully failed him as he could no longer fend for his growing family outside a regular job. "What If Jesus Were Aborted?" is a 174- line poem that joins the abortion argument and posts optional scenarios of various historical personages.

The Mandela theme returns in "And Mandela Inspires" which queries poor administration in the poet's native land and ties his personal challenges of the time to the Mandela sacrifice. "Our Living Men Are Dying" is almost a dirge written after Mandela's death, bemoaning the 'passing' of Africa's best icons. "And Saint Mandela Arrives" is a eulogy to Mandela while "The Legacy He Left" is a fitting epilogue to Mandela and what he represented. "Mandela My Example" actually shows that the poet has learnt the ropes.

In straddling the African socio-political landscape through three stages of maturation, the poet demonstrates an uncanny ability to maintain a passion-sustained focus so rare in distracting economies and tumbling social conditions that his country, Nigeria offers.

Mandela: Echoes Of Apartheid And Impunity compels attention. Now and again it reads like a lamentation which it is not. At other times, one gets the impression of a protest, but it is not one; yet sometimes, the poems read like a realistic offering, and they are not. The immediacy of the subject, the range of the linguistic vehicle, and the varied approach to the presentation of the theme invite a closer reading of the poems. Sam Madugba is indeed a poet of exceptional talent.

I like it; you will too, I think.

Professor Toni Duruaku
Department of English
Alvan Ikoku Federal College of Education
Owerri.

Preface

Mandela: Echoes Of Apartheid And Impunity is a selection of Black African nationalist poetry written by Dr Sam Madugba, some dating from the 1980s when the author was yet a student and spanning more than two decades.

Some celebration of the author's heroes – political, academic and literary in a list that includes some of Africa's most famous. Of all of them, Nelson Mandela evokes his greatest admiration and it is no wonder that the selection begins with Mandela and Apartheid and almost ends with Mandela's funeral.

Thus we have a book shot through with rage against the various forms of the humiliation of the black man by the white man. Whether it is Mandela's struggles, Abortion, HIV/AIDS or Racism or the Mosquito (that necessary evil, that enemy friend, that defender of the black race in West Africa), the absence of any African native tongue as a lingua franca in Africa or the home made tyranny by African rulers, or author's own bitter experiences in the hands of Nigerian civilian despots, whatever is the subject, it becomes for the author an object of rumination, of lamentation and of resentment against the injustice perpetrated by white upon black, by black upon black or the celebration of those who have fought against it or made great sacrifices in that fight or especially Mandela who did so consistently and in a way triumphantly, on a moral higher ground that few in all human history ever could mount.

The reader need not bother, if now and again, the poet, taking poetic license, somewhat presumptuously declares Christ's Apostolic Church "now apostasy-threatened at the top" or campaigns for the canonization of the non-Catholic or even non-believing Mandela. One can only say in charity "Quandoque Homerus dormitet": Sometimes Homer nods. But the zeal is the thing and the innocence is excuse enough.

> Professor (Msgr) Theophilus Okere
> President, Whelan Research Academy For Religion, Culture & Society
> Catholic Archdiocese of Owerri
> Imo State
> Nigeria.

Table of Contents

SECTION A

Mandela: Echoes Of Apartheid And Impunity

Before I Matriculated

'There are so many Hitlers in Africa today
There are so many mercenaries
Ruling Africa today
Some in Botswana
Some in Namibia
Some in Soweto
Some in Zimbabwe
All over Africa
Tormenting my people
Killing my people
Enslaving my people
Victimizing all of us
We've been calling all the world
To help us to fight…'

-Sonny Okosuns

Holy wars

Apartheid: Chants of Liberation

They fell on us
from nowhere.
Their colour told us
their bearing.
5.   From up they must be
above the Sahara and all
we reasoned.

With long nose hooked and barbed
They migrated downwards
10.   across seas and sands
like starved locusts
and behind them lay
a soothing climate.

Poised we saw they were
15.   for the green terrain
of the gentle Veldt.
They stole in like beggars.
Pity enveloped our faces.
Our boundless hospitality indeed -
20.   that resident care for strangers
that forms innate alignment
with our unracialized blood -
became expressed pronto!

We extended arms of welcome
25.   to them – the famished migrants
for quiet and innocent they appeared
land colossal, we reasoned again -
thanks to our Veldt.

This we relinquished uncompelled
30.   for their 'transient' occupation
for their 'sight-seeing' expedition.
They did themselves introduce.
Afrikaaners they ventured
Our unsuspicious faces brightened
35.   with new-found ethos of similarity.
Africans welcome Afrikaaners!
May be distant relations, these are
with skins softened by temperate times.
The strangers settled secure.
40.   No penny charged.
And we saw gratitude dance on their faces,
But lo! this deceived us
For in their hearts,
Smouldered hatred unprovoked
45.   against us, the good hosts.

They talked not much indeed
Lest they reveal their intention.
We minded not
as we let their jaundiced buttocks
50.   plaster on free African seats.
Soon they discarded their travellers' kits!
Soon they multiplied
looking expansionist -
acquiring lands as they saw.
55.   yet we watched with unraised brows-
we gormandized the insults
for aplombic of our future we were
sure – strangers must go
sure – *Agaracha*[1] must come back.
60.   We continued to recline on those chairs

with tobacco pipes betwixt our teeth
as we witnessed our coloured visitors-
tilling our land *sans* permission
sans courtesy
65.   *sans* respect
Acquisition - gradually,
Expansion - unhurriedly,
Replication – uncontrollably,
Domination – ferociously.
70.   Yet we moped
like statues carved from *uha*[2]
affected by rots.
Our gods kept silent
immobilized – hypnotized- bemused
75.   as dear strangers raped
lands kept in their care!

Then staff changed hands
from host to guest.
The mantle of ownership
80.   twined with leadership
crossed carpets dangerously
as the strangers began to direct
the affairs of our land.
With hands of iron grossly cane-stuffed
85.   they chase us about
they abuse our hospitality
they misconstrue our gentility
yet we expected sunlight
after a transient downpour.

90.   We scurried about in confusion
like serpent-pursued rabbits.

No hole was able to cover us
our kraals gave way
to the jackboots of the whites -
95.   the ingrates
the impostors
the usupers.
We were drenched by rain,
thoroughly bedraggled and bedewed,
100   our bodies and eyes became.
Our fathers killed in cold blood
in their thousands
just for doing good.
Yet the Samaritan was eulogized!

105   We became exasperated
though we built around tomorrow.
Our passion gulleyed our cheeks.
Our ribs betrayed their cage.
Our tummies exposed our guts
110   We wondered aloud -
Why, stranger, why?
The unspoken answer evident
though-
our weather, yes, agreeable
115   like his Mediterranean.
Our land, gravid with minerals -
The magnetic effect altogether
of the green-carpet Veldt
spectacular
120   What then of Johannesburg?
Yes, immense Johannesburg….
fraught with yellow rocks
of weighty background value.

125

Would you then blame him
for his actions against us,
the sun-darkened uncivilized hosts?

Bold hand-writing we read.
Bold approaches we made
to our strange guests,

130

no harm at all we meant.
Our wish solely was
to become partners with him
in our soil control.
He refused.

135

He barked eloquently
dry threats oiled with action
from the barrels of hardware,
but we had nothing in return,
the stranger's safety guaranteed.

140

Ian Smith, Voster and Botha –
those horrendous names in history
the serpents of darkness
whose heads remain unlocatable
as they venomize us.

145

To consolidate his new estate -
our papa's land....
the Boer allied with the West
his brothers in oppression
and soon arms and ammunition

150

stranger than the stranger
inundated our land
from America and Europe.
We froze into our shells
But with unprotected defiance

155   harmless placards
we challenged -
and this singular venture
cost us our heritage
as our presence anathemized our land.
160   These strangers –
the Boers, the Afrikaaners, the serpents
soon threw their race on us
and we were to learn
that some races descended from heaven
165   on Ascension Day,
and this maddening egotism
soon bore a child –
they named him Apartheid.

Apartheid grew rapidly
170   unlike most Africa sons
and soon gave the Boer
his independence
and super-power posture.

We were then made naked
175   like the virgin pin.
They sat on the Hottentos.
They defecated on the Ndebeles.
They stole all our farms.
And for a century or more
180   we groaned in agony.
Our skins peeled under *koboko*[3]
Our sweats - warm red syrup -
Our pains we bore with equanimity.
Our groans failed to reach heaven.

185 When nineteen-sixty came....
we marched in protest
hoping for relief
or at least an understanding.
But what did we get?
190 Raw sparks of machine gun
and we perished in hundreds
like fried nuptial termites.

The blacks then Sharpvilled
by blood of fallen brothers
195 decided against further peace
as solution to Apartheid.
Gallantry only we knew
could rescue us from Apartheid –
from humiliation suffered
200 in papa's land.

Then many patriotic fronts
sprouted out of our midst.
Pan-Africanism emerged.
It spread large wings
205 to shelter us from the rain.

The Boers' violence uncalled –
The Boers' bitterness unjustified
came in whirl-wind ferocity
ANC, SWAPO, and other fronts
210 condemned and later abrogated
and their leaders incarcerated or shot.
Steve Bikko, the dogged fighter –
brutalized to submission
to the enforced overtures

215   of a hesitant death.
Nelson, Brave Son, Mandela –
shut away in Pollsmore
for two score and more years.
And critical writers got the axe,
220   but stone-drunk
with the rum of nationalism
they drummed on tireless –
Dennis Brutus
Ngugi Wa Thiongo
225   Kenneth Kaunda and others,
others sang, chants of liberation –
Miriam Makeba
Sunny Okosuns and Bob Marley
Against Apartheid,
230   the crime against humanity.

In the quagmire of chastisement
from partial judiciary…
our tongues continued to wag
against this ignoble outrage
235   which Apartheid represented.
Oh Soweto in 'seventy-six!
Your streets were baptized
with juvenile blood of your sons
for daring the monster.

240   Somehow then the wax fell off
Africa's large ears
and these picked the wailings
cryings and gnashings
from tramplings and stabbings

245 of her children
 by the whiteman
 in the bottom of Africa.
 She proffered diplomacy -
 no way, the Boer shunned
250 in his insensitivity
 and utter perversion,
 and this perversion aroused the world
 as United Nations cried wolf,
 The wolf bearing Resolution 435.

 From the pulpit Apartheid got the lash.
 Yet the Boer remained unperturbed
 waxing an igneous-like hardness
 as he offered the excoriation pill
 to any voice with black body.
260 Laws malignant and malicious
 emerged to restrict us
 and all freedom denied
 all rights violated
 with repeated emergency state declarations.

265 Like the millipede, we perish daily -
 the sons of the soil bake dry
 in flames set by the stranger.

 We sigh. We spit.
 But no spittle came.
270 Our bodies metamorphosed
 into bullet-stopping sand drums-
 all to silence us
 and silence us for ever!

But rejoice a little, brothers!
275   Exalt ebony skin!
Our hidden light may soon appear
as the racists' enclave thins
with a chronicle of nascent liberations.
Talk of Zimbabwe today!
280   Rise, Africans, rise!
Let's wrest Namibia tomorrow
from the Boer.
Then only can we confront Apartheid.
They think we lack the teeth
285   to bite off their ears.
They forget Africa parades-
The Ojukwus
The Adekunles
The Amins
290   the Ghadafis
The Danjumas
-all battle-tested statesmen.

But dear brothers dear
We tarry!
295   for a just war is possible
Western opinion irrespective
since it proffers 435
to discourage us -
for how can dog eat dog?
300   but will Apartheid last for ever?
Let's send fast then,
a ship of rescue
for our brothers still maimed.
Our help they surely need

305   Look! They limp awkwardly.

           Run! Rheotorics run away!!
           For today is action day -
           the books are pregnant
           and radio houses heavy
310   with tales of Apartheid.
           Let's now reclaim Africa
           from Cape to Cairo.
           Let's restore our brothers' breath.
           They are suffocating-
315   they are moaning-
           they are depressed.
           Our redemption we know,
           can only come from us.

           So, chant up, brothers
320   this new song of liberation
           all over Africa.
           Yell out this lovely tune
           with wet eyes skywards
           all over this sun-darkened
           continent.

(Written in Owerri on 25/7/1985 and culled from a book of poems, *Apartheid: Chants of Liberation,* published in Owerri when author was a house officer at the General Hospital, Owerri)

1. Agaracha (Igbo) - the wanderer
2. Uha (Igbo) - vegetable plant
3. Koboko (Hausa) - horse-whip

We groaned in agony
Our skins peeled under *koboko*
Our sweats - warm red syrup
P. 8, lines 180 -182

The Misty Future

How will it look?
How shall we receive it?
What mouths or hands
Shall tell the tale
5.   Of liberation
And safety?
Africa entire dives beyond
The gripping hands of the locust.
My people peel off at last
10.   The jaundiced skin of infiltrators
Who for years stand raping, debasing
And looting our pregnant land-
And with tight-fixedness of teeth
We're bounced to explosion
15.   Like melon sighing off decay
Whose water-soaked children
Are invited by the mills.
How bright will our sun shine?
How sonorous shall the lyrics
20.   Of deserved but held-back freedom
Be?
The re-acquisition of a desecrated heritage!
How melancholic like vinegar-drunk
Irish or Israeli
25.   Will the face of the Boer be?

Go, tell it to the blue waters of Africa
And the Lord Kilimanjaro *et al*
That we'll soon be impatient
The load is ponderous so!

30.   Our ringed necks compressed
        Near now to crackling point
        Meandering wrinkles colonize our faces.
        Won't there ever be retrospective *tête-à-tête*?
        Rescue brothers, rescue fast,
        Before befalls us, the inevitable.

(Written in Owerri on 14/7/1985 and culled from a published *Apartheid: Chants Liberations*)

Your Voice Echoes

Your voice echoes
On the shores of Africa
Crushed black children of today.
Your anguished scream
5   Has Heaven reached.

Cry thus ceaseless
And fight the noble fight
Relentless.
For I perceive the invisible army
10   Invincible
Warming up for assault
On the heartless Boers
Who roast your raw flesh
In large ovens they stole from you.

15   Raise your voice louder then
And chant liberation songs
Like Israelites –
As they encircled Jericho.
Expect you a miracle!
20   For nigh indeed
Your emancipation is.
Your misery will surely evaporate.
But tough moments like now
Will surely climax
25   The nap-catching transition.
The Boers will inherit your wail
As Africa swims clear entire.

Don't then tire out.
Get the voices echoing
30   Like rain-visited crickets
On the curved banks
Of the black oceans.

(Written in Owerri on 17/1/1986 and culled from an unpublished volume, *Nigeria Can Now Marry And Other Poems*)

Their Game Spoils

Aged and vengeance-ridden hands
Dragged a hopeless me behind
Like the sacrificial lamb.
Then closed the only inlet
5   To the *cul-de-sac*
After a heated quarrel
Oiled by unrhymed
Political arguments.

I saw a helpless me
10   Amidst a malice-sworn company
Opened up, then, my mouth, yelling
For paternal protection
Like a mother-pursued child.

That very beast sitting
15   On my prone-lying back
Lifted my head
And violated my well designed right pinna
With tobacco-stained incisors.
Continued I my yell to earthly kin
20   No outlet, it finally dawned
No kicking of legs –
Threats galore –
To send the stubborn to the backyard –
No kicking of arms –
25   For the number, sea shells
And the grips, iron.

Lo! Behind the target
With sun still kissing the ground,
Ran and cried a matchet
30   Across the friction
Of a dormant stone.

Ended that pulsating act
With the decapitator approaching from the rear.
My long assumed confidence
35   Of breaking the resolve
Of the most unyielding of hearts
Took wings at last
After the plea-deafened ears
Looked resolved still
40   To accomplish the task.
Saw I then the futility
Of o'er-confidence.
Yet my disappointed mouth roared
Like a snared lion.

45   Just at the nick of time
As the lightening knife-bearing hand
Descended to strike,
Awoke so my first self
Sprawling on my couch
50   Though dismembered by slumber.

I then realized fast,
The folly of earthly dependence,
For that GREAT HAND it was
That spoiled the vandals' game.

55 Though uninvited, came
  And rescued with precision
  A doomed me.

  Know I this night
  His silent presence
60 Ubiquitous and omnipotent
  As to cause my timely varnishing
  Like an unclenched fist
  From the hands of murderers.

  Chant then, my song, like Job
65 Or should I say
  Our once drenched Zimbabwe
  For reassured I'm once more
  That my Redeemer liveth.

  Miraculous indeed, my salvation was
70 So will those Boer-battered
  Sons of Africa be freed
  To the bemusement
  Of the blacks' detractors.

  Turn then black skin,
75 Your uncoloured eyes skywards
  For there will your help come
  Like mine this night,
  For otherwise

Dawn would have greeted
80 A suppine carion
Of a patriot and poet
Infested by *rigor mortis*[4]
Due to an unreturned second self.

(Written @ No. 88 Zander's Street, Owerri on 3/2/1986 and culled from unpublished *Nigeria Can Now Marry And Other Poems*)

4. Rigor mortis (Medicine) – stiffening of dead bodies a while after death

But For Noble Mosquito

They disturb my sleep
And weaken my red cells
Causing anaemia
From endemic malaria.

5.   But for noble mosquito
The war front would've been
At the left curve of Africa
There'd've been no partitioning
Into political entities
10.   But simply, West Africa.

Our cocoa and palm oil
Plus our innately refined petroleum
- Could've turned Joha'burg's gold.
But would the human race
15.   Have heard our voice?
Would frontline states
Have Angolaed and Zimbabwed Nigeria?
Would Zimbabwe have Harared Lagos?
O how tribalised, I think,
20.   Would our local fronts have been!

(Written in Owerri on 1/8/1986 and culled from an
unpublished volume, *A Stream of Sunlight Thrusts*)

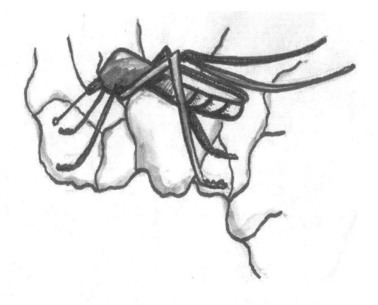

But for noble Mosquito
the (Apartheid) war-front would've been
at the left curve of Africa
P.23, lines 5 - 7

With Them I Protest

Jealousy has eaten you up!
You begrudge me of the sparse Savannah
Bedecking my chin.

Leave them alone, I plead
5.   for I know their number
and what they do for me.

Why not focus on Castro Fidel,
or our own Ojukwu
giants of total protest and wisdom
10   smeared with the Rain Forest Belt bush,
with which they rebel
though China's Mao Tse Tsung
and anti-Apartheid Nelson Mandela
have shown that activism and radicalism,
15   may not have been born
wrapped in beards.

Now, leave them for me, I plead again,
these exiguous children of mine
though he-goat-like they may make me
20   but with them I protest.
With them I profess and pontificate.
I consult them at difficulties.

(Written in Owerri on 2/8/1986 and culled from the
unpublished *A Stream Of Sunlight Thrusts*)

but with them I protest….
I consult them at difficulties
P. 25, lines 20 - 22

Let's Let Loose

This hybrid product
From intercourse
Between the coloured races
And the black -

5.   This brilliant blend
Emerging from such experiments
Arm me with sunny smiles.

Can we then inquire further?
Wouldn't our world have been
10.   Better for it
Should we push-up these cross-pollinations?

A glance at the world boxing rings
Football field and tracks
Reveals the domineering presence
15.   Of black skin, bones and brawns
With white brains
To demolish pure temperate stocks
And even raw tropical valour.

Why can't we then
20.   Let loose these restrictions
On our eager youths
To inundate the world with completeness?
Then would there be no need
Of strangulating racial doctrines

25.   In the buttocks of Africa today…
       Which have denied the globe
       Of beauty
       And fortified youths.

(Written under the Gmelina Tree at Orlu Road/Works Road Junction, Owerri on 8/8/1986 and culled from unpublished *A Stream of Sunlight Thrust*)

Wouldn't our world have been
better for it, if we 'encourage'
these white/black cross-pollinations?
P. 27, lines 9 - 11

I Dined With Africa

Place you spots on it.
I mean the bloated,
Serrated-edged,
Seven-like landmass,
5   Maybe on paper by the artist.
Note then that the workshop
Drew souls from the four cardinals
And even the centre
All black –
10   Black Africans -
Blackness
The pride derived from the resident sun
The colour smeared with beauty
Resilient to age
15   Ever young and ever shinning
With ebony radiance.

I dined with Africa
I dined with them all
But the pepperless broth
20   Continued to discomfort my tongue
Mouth set aglow
Gapped teeth opened
To inhale hissing air
Gum and all, charred
25   Eyes bedraggled
Nose streaming -
For black skins and gums despite –
Snow-white dentition in spite of –
Our tongues refused to rhyme

30   Our breaths refused to resonate
        Twenty and one brothers together,
        Forty and two tongues apart.

        See, we're forced to discuss
        In the tongue of the amber skin
35   The owner of the Union Jack
        Our tormentor of old –
        The cause of our sorrows -
        The supporter of Apartheid -
        See, we betray our intentions
40   Helpless, to allow communication.
        But Africans
        Can't we try one tongue
        Dominant in Africa
        So as to fortify our bond?

(Written in WHO Office Yaba, Lagos on 18/9/1986, and culled from an unpublished volume, *Sakumstantial Verses*)

SECTION B

Mandela: Echoes Of Apartheid And Impunity

As A Medical Student 1986-1992

'Until the colour of a man's skin is of no more significance than the colour of his eyes, there will be war.'

- Bob Marley
Rastaman Vibration

My Friends

People I love
Confident group –
Dominant species –
Big guys –
5   Rebellious patriots –
Those that carve nobility
From the crust of nothingness.
My friends strive.
They snatch greatness
10   From the jaws of simplicity.
The look up to the sky always.
They ever rise after paroxysmal falls
My friends are like the cosmopolitan taxi
No discipline are they restricted to
15   For gifted in all horizon
They all are-
They batter their careers to submission
And get a good harvest
Of deliberate cross-pollination.

20   All tough guys are friends-
So long as they love Nigeria-
My best friend.
My friends so remain
The towering Owelle Zik
25   The stateman who continuously
Oiled the hinges of politics with honesty,
Betrayed Buhari (wherever they put him),
The mover of work and men,
Misunderstood Ojukwu.

30   Misconstrued Nzeogwu *et al,*
        Lyrical voiced Sir Warrior
        We have nobody except you.
        Valiant Ebitu,
        Genius - uncompromising - our pride.

35   Wole, Sir, Soyinka, my Iroko and my candle
        Our own very Achebe
        Your pen made Mr. Nylon Head look small
        Our own Segun Odegbami

40   Golden, Flying and Green Eagles
        Past, present and potential.
        Oh Dele Giwa!
        Oh victim of the coward's envelope!
        Oh Vatsa Mamman, soldier-poet!
        A hapless duo.
        Great Gani F. is my friend
        So is cunning Ray Ekpu
        Who the cap fits
        Rebellious patriots at work.

50   Foreign friends I have too
        Legends in trio-
        Prolific Jimmy Cliff
        The voice that kept Reggae's head above water
        Agile Mohammed Ali
55   The butterfly that bailed ban-haunted boxing
        Oh Pele,
        The footballer's footballer.
        I love Fredrick Forsyth
        The most in-depth espionage weaver,

60   John Paul the second:
     The demystifier of the shrouded papacy.
     Demised Einstein A. in love remains
     The liberator of overpowering energy
     From invisible speck atom.
65   Nelson Mandela inspires as he suffers in Pollsmore.

     My friends can't but include
     My little pets-Felicia and Charlie,
     Marcel, Area, Dem Felly and Bethel
     The freest six souls I've ever seen.

70   I've always loved women
     With gapped white teeth, black gum
     And upright legs, calfless.
     Intelligent ones like young Stella Chuke
     Who combine erudition with belief
75   In man's sovereignty over woman
     Can't but remain dear friends-
     Understanding ones like Joy
     Jealous ones like absconded Pricil
     Struggling ones like sweet Getty
     Prattling ones like our own Chioma
     Little children…
     Sweet things…
     My friends.

(Written in Umueze Umuhu, my village, on 31/7/1987 and culled from the unpublished *Sakumstanshial Verses*)

The Thorn Here Is Sharper

Pursue not solution
To distant Apartheid
Stone-deaf countrymen!
Mobilize yourself
5   Blind peasants!
And dare them here.

The turmoil in the buttocks
Of struggling Africa
Is child's play
10   To our dehumanization
In the hands of brothers here
Kitted and armed by our sweat –
Who starve us
To guard themselves.

15   The thorn here is sharper, brothers
The unfreed fight not
For others' freedom.

(Written in Umueze Umuhu on 18/4/1988 at the height of Babangida's tyranny and misrule and culled from an unpublished volume, *This One Branch Withers*)

ISBN: 978-37146-8-5 P. 88

The turmoil in the buttocks
of struggling Africa is a child's play
to our dehumanization in Nigeria
P. 38, lines 7 - 11

And Mandela Persists

Your persistence, Mandela
calls to question –
are you a man like us?
Nearly a generation
5   now it is
you're confined
by share black pride –
by your noble cause -
You stay behind bars –
10   in dark rooms
like the film negative –
…but can your eyes
adjust again to light?
All because of a stubborn
15   resistance to be cowed
to accept falsehood and puppetry.
But here we crow
after a little deprivation.
Teach us, Mandela
20   to bear pains like you,
Will that your flesh be cannibalized
After breath fails
For we need to eat you,
to adopt your valour!

(Written in University of Nigeria, Enugu Campus, UNEC
as 2nd year medical student on 1/6/1988 and culled from
the unpublished *This One Branch Withers*)

__Denials__

Were it not for Pollsmore –
that tall prison gate –
Mandela, brave son,
would a proud father
5   of many more tall African sons be –
but the accursed Boers deny –
and his seeds
separated from Winnie's eggs
waste in life time
10   and all nature's goodness go.
How can the whiteman pay?
How can he appease
desecrated Africa?

(Written in UNEC on 2/6/1988 and culled from the unpublished *This One Branch Withers*)

I Look Beyond it

This giant hurdle
Called 2nd MBBS
Mounts majestic…
Like an aggrieved colossus
5   Separating me
From a subsequent acquisition.
But thank God
I look beyond it
As I elevate my eyes
10   Skywards to seek help.
The reflected rays from there
Surely pick up my apparatus
And many more acquisitions.

So shall Africa entire
15   Loosen the guilty grip of the Boer
And the queer Apartheid monster
Long raving on with violence
In the South
Of our beautiful continent
20   And denying our good people
Their freedom.

(Written in UNEC on 8/10/1988 when the author, as a 3rd-year medical student, prepared for his 2nd MBBS exams and culled from an unpublished volume, *Campus Fancies)*

<u>Try A Visit Today</u>

      Ever thought of that man
      hidden like Mandela
      though much more longer
      behind the closed door
5.   of every tabernacle -
      beckoning and inviting
      you and me?

      Ever mused over
      His home-thrust enslavement -
10.   a stance He took
      for our company sake?
      Chei[5]*!* how lonesome can one be!

      Ever visited His quiet presence
      a presence very much serene
15.   like a graveyard at night?

      Try a visit today, I plead,
      and confer with Him.
      You'll find Him homely
      and His voice fills the mansion

20.   Try a visit today
      and give Him brief company
      and you must, I promise,
      leave utterly satisfied
      and not unaccompanied

(Written in Umueze Umuhu as a 4th year medical student on 29/12/1989 and culled from a published volume of poems, *The Contract* (*My Appreciation of The Christian Doctrine*)

   5. Chei! (Igbo) - exclamation of despair

Ever thought of Christ
hidden like Mandela
though much more longer
in every tabernacle
P. 43, lines 1-5

SECTION C

Mandela: Echoes Of
Apartheid And Impunity

As A Medical Doctor

'The wheels of justice have a way of grinding falsehood to dust, though they may grind slowly.'

- Ray Ekpu
Newswatch

And Mandela Emerges

Like Christ and hell
the gallows of Pollsmore
had no permanent belly
for its innocent victim.
5   The Boers' intention
to persecute
to intimidate
to frustrate
the brave Mandela
10   Africa's true son
into incarceration-induced suicide
failed even before it began-
not even serial Tuberculosis
forced on him by dank prison walls
15   could let hope die.
And suddenly now-
our Mandela emerges
from the Island of Roben
piercing through the earth
20   like the brave plumule-
like Christ-
towards expected ascension.

(Written in Owerri on 5/11/1992, as a house officer in
General Hospital, Owerri and culled from an published
volume, *Last Days In UNEC*)

And Mandela Ascends

It is only among the Igbos
of Nigeria, East,
that rights activists
are blighted like the moth,
5   singed to crippleness
By kerosene over-flown wick fire
hence parrots of freedom
hardly reach the top here.

10   Our Yoruba brothers-
not even one
yes, not even one-
Awolowo,
Bola Ige
15   Jakande
Ajasin-
ever tasted the salty water
of gubernatorial power
without first tasting
the bitter sap of incarceration
20   following deliberate rebellion
against the tormentors
of their people
no matter the lure,
for to them
25   the prison is a classroom
that teaches leadership and service.

Mandela, even though
the model personae
of this modern world

30   has this innate African spirit of service
        soaked in mud and blood.
        But has the crown
        not always followed the cross?
        Did our Christ not fall
35   three times it was
        under the ponderous gibbet?
        And where is he now?
        Who, but who
        shall stop Mandela
40   from pontificating in Pretoria
        Post-Pollsmore?

(Written in Owerri on 7/12/1994 and culled from the
unpublished *Last Days in UNEC*)

A Passion To Intervene

Love is to intervene
as hatred
or indifference rages.
Justice is but intervening
5.   to right wrongs
to individuals and society.
Speaking the truth is intervention
to clip the wings of falsehood.

Love, Justice and Truth
10.   siblings of Equity
offspring of Peace
trademarks of Integrity-
and these the fool loathes.

Love, Justice and Truth
15.   the most threatened of all virtues
for they singly or in combination
derail the course of the wicked,
the godless, the vandal
who inundate our land.

20.   But one guy gathers the garb of passion
to intervene
ever perfervid to challenge
to save love, justice and truth
from determined extinction
25.   at terrible tortures
over long years
as every available prison embraces
as successive regimes glee in hate.

Gani Fawehinmi
30.   love-monger, justice-seeker
truth-peddler
know ye now and ever
you remain our saint uncanonized
for like Christ,
35.   you continue to give everything
to the ingrates,
and like Socrates
you continue to sermonize
with your unearthly courage.

40.   You embrace avoidable suffering and death
for the cause of truth
just like our own Mandela.

(For Gani Fawehinmi, written in Owerri on 11/3/2003 and culled from the ANA Award-winning volume of poems, *Nigeria: Buhari's Boots, Babangida's Boot's,* published in 2005)

Gani Fawehinmi embraced all sufferings
for the cause of the truth
like our own Mandela
P. 51, lines 40 – 42

AIDS And Africa

Now and then.
the whiteman's burden of inventions
threatens the blackman.

Today, his HIV
5   said to have been aimed
at the hearts of black prisoners
of the Yankee-land
lands in a bow-like trajectory,
10   on the innocents of Africa.

Yesterday, 'twas his chain of injuries -
slave trade,
his government of minority over us -
colonialism,
15   neo-colonialism
with imposition of mediocrities
and serial sponsorship of *coups*,
today, 'tis the affliction
of the majority
with his AIDS virus
20   and our people perish progressive
as we can't but create markets
for his anti-AIDS drugs-
to fecund his economy.
Now, our Mandela lost some sons
25   to this whiteman's substitution weapon
of his pet Apartheid,
now no African family comes spared
by this midday Armageddon.

Now tell me-
30 Had there been an old hurt
by the black skin
against the white?

(Written in Owerri on 6/6/2004 as author co-ordinated
Imo State HIV/AIDS Control Programme)

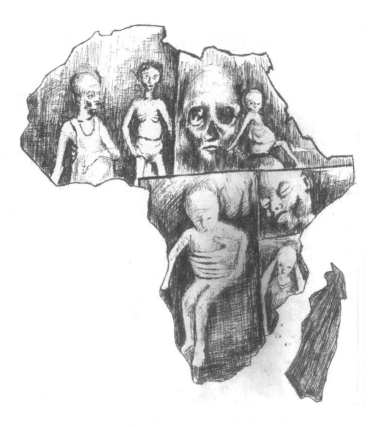

Now no African family comes spared
by this midday AIDS Armageddon
P. 53, lines 27 - 28

The Unnormal Crusader

I'm that prisoner
outside the bars of goal.
Eyes recruited to oversee me
stay uncaring, casual and distant even
5   after all, he has been emasculated.

I got no trial at all -
though the jaundiced verdict
of the fawning kangaroos
remained expected
10   for the trouble maker -
The day-dreamer.
Is he the only one we hurt?
Stupid seeker of just society -
and for this leaning-
15   the idiot declared a strike
and for seven moons and four days
held hostage our fantastic state
as ten and eight sick homes got grounded
and but for our forced acquiescence
20   nearly neatly derailed the second term
longly sought after
for which blood, blue and red, flowed.

Now a recast, a review:
Did he really the strike declare
25   or led he only
a fractured union decreed strike
after Nero neglected negotiations?
And they said they hated this choice of a strike
as their docile people
30   had to suffer.

No effort did we spare
though surreptitious
most, capricious-
to enlist him.

35   We even used his subjects on him
but the poor bastard snubbed and scorned.
He wanted no money, nor position
He wanted justice for those he represented.

Three times did we attempt
40   to snuff him out
as we are wont to,
three times did he escape unhurt.
A miracle, perhaps!
or like Uwazuruike,
45   he did also visit India!

But we own society.
Like Nero, this world is ours.
We impoverish all
to compel loyalty.
50   But this unnormal crusader persists
and like Mandela, rejects compromise.
Pay my colleagues, he insisted!
He really made us sweat, those days.

But who are your colleagues, young man?
55   Who would you die for?
Those traitors without livers?
Those saboteurs?
How can you alone change Nigeria
Decadent with debts, dirts and bribes?

60   Adamant and defiant, he went.
      Okay, since he wears immortality
      serve him the starvation pill
      afterall, Awo did that try against Biafrans.
      His post - Yes, his peculiar post?
65   but he is a genius.
      The best we have here.
      Loyalty and not service, my man!
      Who's talking of bests?
      Post him out! Idiot!
70   But is justice demanded disloyalty?
      Now the mad man cares not even!
      Deprivations affect him not!
      Make it total therefore -
      His job!
75   Sack him!!
      His colleagues, after all, have sold out
      and like Judases, you know
      most are dogs around our table.
      Look, we've seen him through-
80   No brother, no friend
      No big sister even -
      Nobody to speak for him -
      he is a man alone -
      a prisoner outside the cage!
85   Their mistake, you know?
      For an inscrutable force surrounds me
      right from the umbilical cord severance -
      hence humiliations -

ISBN: 978-37146-8-6 P. 139

Like Nero, this world is ours
We impoverish all
To compel loyalty.
P. 57, lines 47 – 49

conspiracies and betrayals incessant -
90 move me not
as I fire on tireless,
like that locust eater of old -

to redirect society.
For the scriptural tonic -
95 ''Be not afraid''
ever in my ears resounds.

I laugh at powerful men -
pigs in bullet-proof vests
buried in mobile coffins
100 impermeable still to bullets
perennially attracted to them
by their vices.

I laugh at politicians, too,
African politicians, the more
105 For God, they are wont to play
with their rather volatile power.

How can we all kowtow
at the feet of nobodies,
Before power-wielding inferiors
110 opportunists
just for bread and butter
communally owned
though they had them seized
as a bait for loyalty?

115 Now democracy has ruined Nigeria
as she begets un-uniformed soldiers

dictators *per excellence*
to inundate our troubled land.

But I'm the prisoner at large
120   I'm loyal only to God and to society
Thus the chastisement of the wicked
can't make me glue-lipped
all these ten and two moons
of tummy size reduction
125   since my source of bread vanished,
not un-anticipatedly, however.

Worst still, the colleagues
for whom I went to war
with whom I remonstrated
130   embraced, rather than repel the foe.
Even my own face
now repels them from afar.
I'm now like one
exiled into the lion's den
135   no more calls to once loved leader
no visitations extended even
from especially
the beneficiaries of my struggle
the witnesses of my courage
140   lest the distant sentinel spot -
lest they be queried
for associating with the dissenter.

At chance meetings even
they marvel that I go not naked yet
145   that I still sing -
that I still write

that I still confront evil
from the house of exile.
But I have them all forgiven
150   for faced with want below
and a murderous dictator above
and without any heart
how can't they disown me?

But society suffers my job loss
155   my forced exit creates a vacuum
ever unfillable.
Four compelled umpires
within twenty and four moons
all unsound, all unprepared
160   fell with terrible bangs,
and so coldly discharged
like expended cartridge
by the uncaring lords.
I remain that tree that makes a forest!

165   Now, no adversity was spared me
all these ten and two moons
of great expectations.

A colleague stupendous with wealth
though utterly miserly
170   saw even the law court
as a let out channel
of his parsimony
just to get me suffer.

And worse still, brother
175   is this persistent increase

in the number of dependent mouths
as flesh-seeking spirits
compete to grace my flagging loin -
so as to be fed with near empty plates
180   in my dreary domain -
in my lonesome stance-
rather than storm the wombs
of the commandeerers' wives -
where our wealth is trapped.

185   Miracle! More miracle!!
As all still see them
these defiant kids of the rebel
go to school
and in their quality classes even
190   they stay atop like their father!
They even wore new clothes last Easter
and ate foreign rice this Christmas.
They get ill
my heart skips
195   but they recover *sans* medicines!
A bee-hive now is my habitation
and ugly loneliness evaporates.

Yes, that steady gaze skywards
at he who dwells above the firmaments
200   it is -
for before the wild storm
my trust in him was in *cent per cent.*
Today, a *mille* by a *mille*
in every life aspect
205   even in guiding the last lump
of limp leaves-stained foofoo

into my large mouth,
now that human trust seems distant.

Now I get me more convinced.
210 A miracle
from the celestial force of my trust
will lift me up sooner or later
from this state of anomie
without forgetting to remember
215 justice to the scoundrels
littered all over Nigeria
who covet common goods
and pour pains persistent
on richly endowed citizens.

220 I shall soon rise, I know
in response to destiny
but not without our people
long chastised, long hurt
by the impostors ever dominant
225 ever brutal
ever conscienceless.

(Written in Owerri on 15/2/2005, about one year after
Udenwa sacked me and culled from the published *Nigeria:
Buhari's Boots, Babangida's Boots)*

The Upright His Ironies

He washes clean his hands
so as to eat with elders.
He then builds a house for money
where money would dwell
5   as they say.
But the elders shared their foods
and he is not given a crust.
Into the house he built even,
money refuses to enter.
10   Love your neighbour as yourself!
So says the holy script.
His neighbours he has openly loved
and sacrificed his life even for,
but their vehement hatred astounds.
15   The truth the holy writ again proclaims,
sets one free.
He has spoken unalloyed truth
His reward, brother,
a chain of bondage
20   in his unrosy house of exile
as all, even direct beneficiaries
desert.
And for his benefit,
the gods broke his waist too
25   as he escaped from foes.
So, he goes about in thought:
are there still other sacrifices to make
to earn food for the family
after all these acceptable efforts?
30   If wealth is a miracle
as his people say

what of three square meals
or taxi money even?
Any ear at the other end of the telephone?

(Written in Amakohia, Owerri on 23/2/2006 about two years after author's sack by Achike Udenwa Government)

What If Jesus Were Aborted?

What if Jesus were aborted
by Mary and Joseph
being a child of hapless circumstances –
a transcendental burden –
5   an atypical cross
planted on the shoulders
of a fore-sworn teenage virgin
betrothed to an unusual man?
Yes, His story wouldn't have been –
10   The 2000-year-old Catholic Faith -
Redemption –
The New Testament!
Surely, the gospel
would've been washed
15   into the drains with Him,
and human captivity by Satan
would've remained permanent!
Gawd! Man would've lost
and become utterly barbaric
20   and Thomas Hobbes' derision in Sheol
Would've been eternal.

What if St Agusutine were aborted?
Terrible!
No *Confessions, Sermo, City of God, et al*
25   knowledge, spiritual and moral
would've been Caspian Sea.
What if Socrates were aborted?
Oh, bye-bye to Anthropocentric Philosophy –
Star, moon and planet-gazing
30   would've been by now,
taught in primary schools.

What if John Paul II were aborted?
Communism would've been standing erect
like *Uzii,* the truth tree
35   and the Papacy's shroud of mystery
would've been thicker and darker.

What if Mother Theresa were aborted?
Man wouldn't've known
that Calcutta could exist
40   around Buckingham's Palace
even as it exists in Ajegunle

What if Martin Luther
And Henry the Eighth were aborted
Christianity would surely,
45   Have been saved
From television acrobats of today
and these pockets of rebellion
in uncompleted buildings and ware-houses.

What if Zik were aborted?
50   Africa and Nigeria
would still have remained
scrambled by colony-seeking Europe
and especially in Nigeria –
a fragment of ethnic nationalities
55   wearing hostility like sweater
would've been our lot,
with the likes of OBJ and IBB
parading noisily and respectively
as local Yoruba and Hausa champions
60   smearing their tiny enclaves
with their scents of putrefaction.

What if Ojukwu were aborted?
perhaps the Igbo
would've avoided today's marginalization
65   having earlier been totally annihilated
in the pogroms of the mid-sixties.

What if Hitler were aborted?
Concentration camps! Nazi!
Genocidal Second World War –
70   Oh, no!
But… but… but wouldn't the world've been better
without Adolf Hitler
Emperor Caesar Nero
Idi Amin and Bokassa
75   IBB and Abacha –
fraternities of blood and hurt, all?

What if Buhari were aborted?
Buhari, the only yardstick, so far –
of civil and fiscal discipline
80   and of course, of political possibility here …
We wouldn't've known
that Nigeria can be governable.

What if Achebe were aborted –
Mr Nylon head would've thought
85   No genius could've emerged
from slavery-desolated Africa.
Now, Soyinka – God forbid!
Gani – A serious issue!
They'd've, without the duo,
90   been hawking us alive like kites –

our enemies in government.

What if Mandela were aborted?
Eclipse of Apartheid would've persisted
in the buttocks of Africa
95   And nascent Vuvuzela experience,
a mirage!

What if Jenner and Ross,
Fleming and Koch were aborted?
Small Pox and Malaria
100   infections and TB
would today be mysteries
attracting sacrifices extortionate
to placate their deity harbingers

What if Newton and Einstein
105   got aborted *in utero*[6]?
Automobiles wouldn't've been,
just as the wails of Hiroshima
would've not been heard.

What if Mohammed Ali were aborted?
110   The feat of Negroid-Caucasians
would've still been in doubt
and Rocky Marciano white noise unending.

What if Jimmy Cliff were aborted?
Reggae would've remained
115   a rumbling of drunks,
lunatics and psychopaths in dreadlocks –
propelled by *wee-wee*[7].

What if Sir Warrior were aborted?
Osadebe, Rex Lawson, Paulson Kalu
120   would've still been wearing
togas of Oriental high-life kings.

What if Michael Jackson were aborted
Oh! Magical Michael Jackson –
The flexible body of songs and dance
125   Celestial Michael Jackson,
the moon-walker on earth!
Lord, it'd've been loss upon loss.
What if Okocha were aborted?
This Brazilo-Nigerian wizard
130   this unprecedented football event
this man of soccer impossibilities
would've been denied the world.

What if Ribadu were aborted?
We would've been saved the sad knowledge
135   that in Nigeria hard work and excellence
come despised and punished.

What if Dora Akunyili were aborted?
Fake drug barons and their reign
would still threaten citizens' lives
140   and Yar'Adua's kitchen cabinet
would've lingered on still

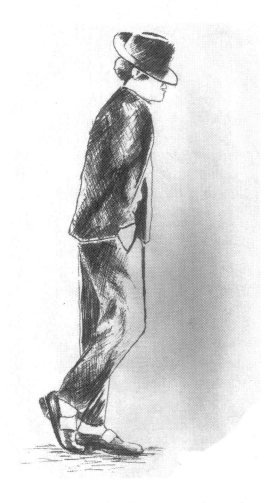

What if Michael Jackson were aborted
Oh! Magical Michael Jackson –
The moon-walker on earth!
Lord, it'dve been loss upon loss.
P. 71, lines 122 - 127

even *post-mortem*[8].

What if Jonathan were aborted?
This Jonathan with good luck –
145   Awolowo in grave
wouldn't have known as he knows today,
that all power comes from God.
Petrol supply would still be
the cartel's Tantalus
150   and Maurice Iwu
would've in tracks been today
warming up
to threaten 2011.
What if I were aborted –
155   - my writing
my singing
- my committed courageous confrontations
of all, no matter!
Drainage-bound? God forbid!
160   But.. but… but.. who would have had
the shoulders
to bear my burdens of pain?
And… and… my patients?

So, Hail thee!
165   Most Holy Catholic Church
Spouse of thy redeeming Lord
who propounded the anti-abortion law
and still propagates and crusades it
century over century –
170   welcome or despised –
to preserve for our earth,
her saints, thinkers,

geniuses, friends and lovers.

(Written in Holy Rosary Hospital, Emekuku on 21/6/2010, during my 4-month stint of penance and purification as a medical consultant in that ancient health centre as I pursued my case in court)

6. In utero (Medicine) – in the womb
7. Wee-wee (slang) – Indian hemp (Cannibis)
8. Post-mortem (Medicine) – after death

What if Okocha were aborted
this Brazilo-Nigerian wizard —
this unprecedented football event
this man of soccer impossibilities
would've been denied the world
(P. 71, lines 128 - 132)

And Mandela Inspires

Mandela's dehumanization
In Pollsmore by the whiteman
turned a dependable experience
when Achike Udenwa
5   of Imo, Nigeria Government House
struck merciless
to terminate my joy.
For I with colleagues medical,
did remonstrate arguably,
10   against his perfidy,
eight whole years it lasted.
Granted,
The first two years
following the sudden disengagement
15   as I vividly had the memory
of my colleagues betraying
of my works of excellence
denied, and even discredited,
of painstaking acts of patience
20   employed by our mother union
as we negotiated as patriots
with the benumbed government -
all to avoid the eventual
seven-month long strike,
25   turned mostly unbearable
as all friends relocated
their loyalty,
as even the home front rebelled
as lurking austerity dared.

30   But did I contemplate suicide
      like Zik in the Yankees' land?
      No, never!
      Neither did I take to despair
      for as the agony of injustice
35   wore on like Apartheid
      in the buttocks of Africa,
      as the unjust triumphed
      as the innocent ate fodders
      meant for the guilty
40   came then, perhaps,
      recurrent relapses into self-blame
      as midday hunger starred.

      Did I go wrong? Where?
      Should I have accepted the bribes
45   And compromised my lore?
      Shouldn't I have placed first
      the growing family before integrity?

      Just then Bibi, reverend sister mine
      descended from Abuja
50   empty-handed as usual and cajoled:
      'Oh, complaining already?
      After just five years?
      You say you love Mandela?
      You recall his days in gaol?
55   Consider you yourself
      more offended than he
      or less qualified for society's pastime?'

      Then I caught me once more
      the long rope of courage

60 dropped down
   light years it was
   from the high windows of Pollsmore.

   So, I ignored the multiple arms of torment
   as I, with my visage of Janus
65 steadily positioned skywards
   continued to challenge
   the power-mongering brute
   at awfuf costs to comfort
   even after his 2007 self-succession
70 by his Peacock shadow
   in our Government House,
   a seat of corruption and arrogance
   which shall soon be proselytized
   into a throne of truth and mercy
75 should we one day occupy it.

   I wore on endless
   like a child being forced Epsom Salt
   as the matter lingered on
   with conspiratorial deliberateness,
80 till victory won in their own court.
   Yes, today,
   seven years after
   David challenged the Goliaths.

(Written in Owerri on 5/7/ 2010 when God helped me recover my job in court as a Daniel chief judge, Paul Onumajuru, gave me victory against a government he served as No. 4 citizen)

Then I caught me once more
the long rope of courage
dropped down from Pollsmore Prison window
(Pp 77-78, lines 58 - 62)

<u>Our Living Men Are Dying</u>

For Alexander the Great
His copulating father it was
that gave him life
while the great Aristotle
taught him how to live.
For us Christians
the teacher of good living
has always been the Christ
through his Apostolic Church
now apostasy-threatened at the top.

But for us Africans
we learnt to live well
even before the gospel's advent
through our resident cultures
and heritages ancestral.

Now our Christians
and animists
come now forgetting their teachers
as paganism of corruption
takes over the classroom,
the pulpit
the moon-light playground
under the very nose
of the civilized whiteman
as his ambulatory virus
corrupts both the Bible and the Ofo[9].

But Soyinka,
a positively eccentric folk ours
long declared the African dead
30   when the only living among them,
Nelson Mandela,
gradually died in Pollsmore
under the jackboot of the white Boer
as Biafran children
35   got Kwashiorkored to suffocation
under the fatigued
and jackbooted Gowon.

With the end of the hostilities
Nigerian –
40   with the end of Apartheid
We thought Africans could begin to live
but did we ever contend
with the Amins, the Abachas,
the Bokassas, the Nguemas, the IBBs -
45   who keep on killing us as we keep mute
in the face of tyranny?

For long, only a few
remained standing –
Ojukwu, Buhari and Mandela
50   Achebe, Soyinka and Dele Giwa
Fela, Gani and Beko
without forgetting our truncated Ubani Chima -
but our living men
now gradually die off-
55   like millipedes
off Africa's landscape
leaving us dead folks

to contend with today's butchers
in togas of democrats -
60   offspring of rabid dictators.

(Written in Owerri on 5/12/2014 as Nelson Mandela
breathed his last in a Pretoria hospital after Dele Giwa,
Fela, Beko, Ubani Chima, Gani, Ojukwu and Achebe
took their not infrequent turns of late)

9.   Ofo (Igbo) – a family symbol of uprightness

And Saint Mandela Arrives

Eternity,
the first quest of the catechumen
at baptism-
though the last attainment
5   after life, death and judgment.
Now recall the tales of Mandela -
that bundle of contentment
after a life
fraught with fulfillment
10   in the bottom of Africa-
after displacing the Boers
with a twenty-seven-year-old weapon
of resistance
against torments of his people
15   in Pollsmore gallows.
-Yes he resisted and persisted
-yes, Mandela emerged
from the dungeon of Pollsmore
after a forced hibernation,
20   conquering his captors-
with a new weapon-
the Calvary weapon of forgiveness.
Then with a head ever unbowed-
Ascended he
25   the seat of power
formerly serially plastered
with jaundiced buttocks
of the migrant Boer.
Later relinquished he power
30   unlike most African pretenders
resisting the lust to self-perpetuate

after reconciling the locusts
with the owners of the land.

Now Mandela basks bountiful
35   in the air of freedom
of victory
of global father-figure posture
before this call to Heavensgate -
for Christ's tragic personae
40   deprived him the praise
deserved by his unnormal victory
over the cross and the grave -
and over the Sanhedrin
as the humble Pointer to the way,
45   appeared He only to His friends
thus depriving his enemies
the expected had-we-known posture,
unlike, the lot of the Madiba
who, ripened by age,
50   tarried on like the vulture
till secured he,
the repentance of his tormentors.

Now accolades poured ceaseless
across the Atlantic, Indian and Pacific
55   from the nylon heads,
the former justifiers
of Apartheid and Pollsmore.
And that very day,
from my tube
60   I watched Obama,
our Americanized brother
soaked in rain

rattle off like an inspired parrot
the eulogies of Mandela
65   amidst a bee-hive
of his co-pretenders.
And all these fallacies of praise
got gladly accepted by Madiba
without his dignity compromised,
70   without his vision ever blurred.
And now Mandela arrives
Heavensgate like Okigbo,
like Achebe Chinua ours.
And all observe him arrive -
75   black and white -
all expect his royal welcome
for fully prepared for paradise
he was
for like Isaac, son of Abraham
80   and Mother Theresa of Calcutta
he obeyed and loved all through
and like Christ the Lord,
sacrificed everything
as he allowed himself
85   to be crushed with protracted quarantine -
with unearthly cruelty
by the whiteman,
brothers of the hard-hearted Jews and Romans
so as to expose to the world
90   the forgiving soul
of the blackman.

Will any Devil's advocate now
emerge to deny
the saintly Nelson Mandela
95   the oil of Canonization
by the Pope,
after everybody's positive verdict?

(Written in Owerri on 15/12/2014 as Mandela is interred
in his Qunu Village, Cape Town, South Africa)

Who will now deny Mandela
the oil of Canonization
after everybody's positive verdict?
P. 86, lines 92 - 97

<u>The Legacy He Left</u>

Had his jailers remained not forgiven
soon after his late release
had he thought of them undeserving,
nothing would've assured his peace

5   Mandela, thou fine figure of Christ
who even in His gibbet-driven thirst
did forgive His guilty executors
and so became the Institutor
of celestial reconciliation
10   not based on terrestrial contrition

Smile on then, Madiba, from heaven
as you watch the globe from galaxy
having acquired a repose uneven
by leaving us this your legacy.

(Written in Owerri on 23/1/2014 as author ruminated
over the events of Mandela's life)

Mandela My Example

Christ in his Church
Is my life
Football, my reincarnation
Medicine is my treasure
5   Poetry, my pleasure
Sacred music is my elevation
Woman, my degradation
Sir Warrior and Jimmy Cliff
Are my relaxation
10   Human rights and justice
My concern
Nelson Mandela is my example
Children, my delight
Teaching is my joy
15   Writing my job
Hard work is my health
And insomnia, of course,
My death.

(Written in Owerri on 12/6/2014 as the FIFA 2014 World
Cup Fiesta kicked off in Brazil and as author breathed his
last on this compelling compilation)

<u>Mandela:</u>
<u>Echoes Of Apartheid And Impunity</u>

partly excerpted from the following works of poetry by
the same author:

1. *Apartheid: Chants Of Liberation,*   published 1993
2. *Nigeria Can Now Marry And*
   Other Poems,   yet unpublished
3. *A Stream Of Sun Light Thrusts,*   yet unpublished
4. *Sakumstanshial Verses,*   yet unpublished
5. *This One Branch Withers,*   yet unpublished
6. *Campus Fancies,*   yet unpublished
7. *The Contract (My Appreciation*
   Of The Christian Doctrine),   published 1999
8. *Last Days In UNEC,*   yet unpublished
9. *Nigeria: Buhari's Boots,*
   Babangida's Boots,   published 2005

Epilogue

Not since after reading Dennis Osadebay's *Africa Sings* in the 1950s have I ever come across a collection in verse of indictments of white imperialism as penetrating as this work: *Mandela: Echoes Of Apartheid And Impunity (Chronological Predictions and Fulfillments)* by Sam Madugba. But beyond Osadebay, it also indicts black tyranny sadistically unleashed against fellow blacks.

The work is a systematic analysis of the pretentious incursion into Africa of white imperialists under all types of guises, the perpetuation of all shade of imperialistic escapades, applying all manners of usurpation. As if that was not enough, fellow black men unleashed native tyranny over their own people, an unexplainable unnatural action about which Kofi Anan, former United Nations' Secretary-General, once commented as follows: "Africans must guard against a permissive self-destructive form of racism that unites citizens to rise up and expel tyrannical rulers who are white but to excuse tyrannical rulers who are black."

In this work, in verse, the point is succinctly made that the evil of apartheid may have extended to West Africa but for the intervention of the great mosquito that halted that iniquitous campaign. The poet also wonders whether mixed breed would solve the world problem. And what of promoting the establishment of one language as a cement to bind the African people, he suggests.

In My Friends, the author recalls those he admires, and they are few, and encompass different areas and disciplines. But insufficiently few of them were not enough to galvanise the people into a mass movement against native tyranny.

His lamentation over native tyranny is heightened by the fact that he finds it in abundance in his own country and among his immediate people.

The author eulogises Mandela, wishing that he taught Africans his trade of resistance, and very metaphorically, wished Africans could eat his body, to generate resistance against imperialism whether white or black.

Can the white man pay for all his misdeeds in Africa, he asks? For example, can he make up for depriving Mandela from having children through his incarceration?

The author compares his medical course with the fight against imperialism, thus implying that it was not easy.

To drive home the esteem in which he holds Mandela, he even goes to the extreme of comparing Jesus Christ in the Blessed Sacrament in the tabernacle with Mandela in confinement. He emphasized Mandela's triumph and ended saying that there can be no crown without a cross. He also admires Yoruba activists, particularly Gani Fawehinmi, whom he describes as love-monger, justice-seeker and truth-peddler and an uncanonised saint.

The work laments over white-created HIV/AIDS. His condemnation of abortion is brilliantly put in his "what if ...were aborted" style of presentation, arguing that the world would have been deprived of many greats (good or bad) had they been aborted. He ended that brilliant presentation by saluting the Catholic Church for opposing abortion uncompromisingly.

The poet did not forget to recall his unforgettable ordeal at the hands of Achike Udenwa, (Governor, Imo State, Nigeria, 1999 – 2007), but thanked God for his rescue through the intervention of a just judge, implying that all is not yet lost.

Sam Madugba's use of apt illustrations to enhance communication where his loads of imagery cannot reach make *Mandela: Echoes Of Apartheid And Impunity* a more complete literary work.

This is a work that is timeless, a work that will defy the present Nigerian generation of non-readers to become the toast of generations yet unborn, as time permits, because "good wine needs no bush."

Emmanuel A. C. Orji
Mmawuru Court,
Orji, Urata.
February 16, 2014.

About the Author

Dr Samuel Iheanacho Madugba hails from Umueze Umuhu in Ngor-Okpala LGA, Imo State, Nigeria. Born September 17, 1961, Dr Madugba, a philosopher and lay theologian, studied Medicine and Surgery between 1986 and 1992 at the College of Medicine, University of Nigeria, to where he returned for his specialist course in Public Health in 2001.

A no-nonsense charismatic leader, crusader of social justice and human rights activist, Dr Sam Madugba's fight for doctors in Imo State Government Service over their unpaid wages led to his premature retirement in 2004, an unjust action he challenged in court and won after 7 years of fierce legal battle.

In 2005, Dr Madugba won the Association of Nigeria Authors, ANA, Imo State Chapter's Award in Poetry with his collection of poems, *Nigeria: Buhari's Boots, Babangida's Boots.* Other published books of Dr Madugba are, *Apartheid: Chants of Liberation, 1993; Obesity Among Nurses (Problems and Solutions), 1996; The Quick Intervention, 1999; The Contract (My Appreciation of the Christian Doctrine), 1999; The Traffickers, 2008,* apart from his published works in learned medical journals and columns in newspapers.

Dr Madugba, a community/church leader was once the Parish Pastoral Council Chairman of St Patrick's Catholic Church, Mbutu-Okohia where he doubled as choirmaster.

Dr Madugba is now a Director in the Public Health/ Primary Health Care Department of Imo State Ministry of Health. He is married to Linda and they have seven growing children.